BEAUTY EXISTS SO CLOSE TO AGONY

Also by R. Clift

TO FEEL ANYTHING AT ALL
TO BE REMEMBERED
TOMORROW WILL BE KINDER

UNTIL WE MEET AGAIN
YOUR THOUGHTS DESERVE A DECENT PLACE TO LIVE
THE POETRY OF WILDFLOWERS: FIELD JOURNAL

BEAUTY EXISTS SO CLOSE TO AGONY

a collection of ekprastic poetry

BY

R. Clift

THE CONSTELLATION POET

LONDON | LIVERPOOL

2022

Copyright 2022 by R. Clift.
All rights reserved.
Published March, 2022.

ISBNs: 978-1-7369665-7-0 (trade paperback),
978-1-7369665-8-7 (ebook)

Cover photo by William Henry Fox Talbot.
Author photo & illustration by Laura Clift.

To Savannah, Laura, Ethan, and Biddy

Ekphrasis (Etymology)

ek·phra·sis | \ ˈek-frə-səs

- *ek*: "out of"
- *phrasis*: "speech or expression"

Ekphrastic Poetry is a conversation between poetry and art. The poet interprets the art and then creates a narrative that represents their reaction to it. It is one of the oldest forms of writing, with its meaning having originated in ancient Greece.

Introduction

This collection of poems was written during visits to the Walker Art Gallery, Lady Lever Art Gallery, Tate Liverpool, Tate Britain, Victoria & Albert Museum and The National Gallery in London during my travels abroad in February 2022.

Ekphrasis poetry was first introduced to me by my late poetry professor, Arthur Smith, years ago. Without him, I would not be the poet I am today. Exploring this ancient form of writing while standing before these artworks for the first time brought out a dynamic, and almost surprising kind of reaction and conversation between myself and the artworks that I believe, wouldn't have happened otherwise if I didn't have a pen in hand.

I rarely title my poems, but these particular poems begged for titles— so I had a bit of fun with it. Each of the titles is a phrase pulled from the museum plaque accompanying the artwork at its respective museum.

For me, this is still a brand new, and perhaps my now favorite way to experience art going forth. I look forward to writing more ekphrastic poems as years go by— and whether you call yourself a poet or not, I encourage you to do the same.

Rachel Clift
March, 2022

VISIT RCLIFTPOETRY.COM TO VIEW THE ARTWORKS
THAT INSPIRED THE POEMS IN THIS COLLECTION

Contents

PIERCED BY HIS ARROW	15
FROM MEMORY	17
ATTRACTED BY HER COMPANY	19
EVE IS SHOWN RECOILING	21
HER REAL NAME WAS AMINA	23
LIKE PIECES OF MUSIC	25
HER FACE HALF-BURIED IN THE ROCKY GROUND	27
SECRET LOVE BETWEEN FATE AND THE ROMAN BOY	29
SHE STRAINS TO HEAR THE MUSIC,	31
IN THE FORM OF AN ANGEL	33
THE 'GRACES' REPRESENTED	35
UNDER THE LIGHT OF THE MOON	39
IN SLEEP, OR PERHAPS IN DEATH	41
WHAT IS REAL AND WHAT IS NOT	43
HIS SO-CALLED 'ROSE PERIOD'	45
THE MUSE, EXTRACTED FROM ANY CONTEXT	47
AN ANGEL SHE CANNOT SEE	49
A STATE OF MELANCHOLY	51
YELLOW WITH HOPE	53
TO FIND HEAVEN	55
EROS CARESSING A BUTTERFLY	57

POEMS

PIERCED BY HIS ARROW

My darling— they blame you, but all
you ever asked for was the truth.

As I gaze at you and you gaze
at the last memory of the one
you so desperately wanted to love—
I can feel it in my bones—

if you were sent back in time,
able to redo that night,
you wouldn't change a thing—

you'd shine a light on his face again
wouldn't you? You'd anger the gods
ten times over to reveal what is real.

You would rather honestly lose
this great passion altogether than
spend the rest of your life loving a lie.

// *Psyche deserted by Cupid*, 1875. George Fredric Watts.

FROM MEMORY

There is darkness in every corner—
I see what looks like
yellow stars on the horizon, the
light blue buds could be
sleeping flowers,
and the reflection of a
soldier— or maybe that's
the old man with heavy footfalls
and loud breath— the
three dark-haired ladies move like
church mice on the wooden floor—
I can barely keep up with where
they stand. In the green and
turquoise shadows I meet
my own eyes— or maybe
the eyes of another
through the looking glass—
trying to make sense
of what is staring back.

// L'île Madre: Clair de Lune, 1908-09. Henri Eugène Le Sidaner.

ATTRACTED BY HER COMPANY

Do you ask for privacy or attention?
Tell me— why did they give you a
curtain— do you fear
the gaze of strangers
or are you shielding
them from your own gaze?
Is this where you always wanted
to spend eternity?
Behind a screen— a mystery— so
whenever it is raised
the whole room
turns their heads and crowds
around— away from Monet and
Pissarro and Seurat and the man who
stole Van Gogh's irises— is this the
power you always longed to hold?
From years of never truly being seen
to this— is this your retribution?
Demanding nothing short of reverence
with your mocking smile.

// *Madame Hessel au Sofa*, 1900. Edouard Vuillard.

EVE IS SHOWN RECOILING

She twists her body away
from the eyes of men
who may perceive her—

Eve, I wish you were taught how
not to shrink— I wish
you were told it wasn't
your fault— you were just
the easiest one to blame.
Known as the temptress, the
downfall, the one who ruined
everything— but if a man
could think for himself— one
could pause & realize that
the blame is not
only yours to bear.

Adam could have said
no.

// *Eve*, 1883. Auguste Rodin.

HER REAL NAME WAS AMINA

Jacob, where is her soul?
You carefully captured and carved
every curl, every curve
of her lips, every contour
of her breast— but where
is the life in her eyes— where
is the knowledge, the emotion,
the fervor in this woman?
You have made the decision to put
her on display and ask
strangers to lay hands on
her bronze shell— but did you
ever ask her if this
is what she wanted?

Where are her regrets, Jacob?

Where is that one thing inside her
that was made to be eternal?
Why hollow her out?
Why immortalize a woman if she can't
even look into your eyes?
Why be so cruel as to give her eternity—
yet blind her of her own humanity?

// *Israfel*, 1930. Jacob Epstein.

LIKE PIECES OF MUSIC

With only nine faint lights barely holding on
to that night sky, it must be one
awfully dark and lonely place for
a bright young star like that to choose to
throw itself into a snow-covered England—
where dreary days stretch themselves
into months and winter seems
as endless as the hour before dawn.

Maybe that little star will feel
more at home here among the
frigid Englishmen— the burning
wood stoves, the void that settles
between the bowing trees at dusk.

Look there, an orange glow
shines below, like a beacon—
for all I know that star is
some wayward angel going home
to visit lost loved ones—
as I turn away
I can only hope that it will be
welcomed in from the cold.

// *The Falling Star*, 1909. James Hamilton Hay.

HER FACE HALF-BURIED IN THE ROCKY GROUND

You hear unfamiliar voices and
a constant murmuration of
the sighs of strangers
as they gaze over you, past you.
The woman in black offers
no sympathy and the men surrounded
by white snow and red curtains are
far too preoccupied to lean over
and offer any words of
respite. After all, you're just another
woman, crackled
green flesh, melting into the
folds of bronze beneath—
there are far too many to
pity— so why even try.
Why waste the time.

They avert their eyes when
walking past and
all I can think to say is
my darling, I'm so sorry.

// *Danaid*, 1885. Auguste Rodin.

SECRET LOVE BETWEEN FATE AND THE ROMAN BOY

He tries, in vain, to gain Fate's
attention, but with only the accuracy
of a shrouded Eros— she is missed
and he, destined
to wear that strained smile
on his lips to hide
the dark hollow in his chest.

There is nothing easy about
love unrequited— in this room
of so many gazing eyes, hands held,
and eternities spent in a tender
embrace— how much is it to ask—
truly— that they may merely see
each other?

How can I tell her that
she does not have to blindly take
her next step off a marble ledge—
if only this stone could
yield once more— that veil
could be lifted, love could be
set free, he could finally turn his head,
and she could be known.

// *Secret Love*, 1876. Antonio Rossetti.
// *Fate-Led*, 1891. Albert Toft.
// *Lupercalia*, 1907. Conrad Dressler.

SHE STRAINS TO HEAR THE MUSIC,

and you can almost make out
the soft note from her
broken lyre— just
as you gaze upon her—
you know exactly how it feels
to be lost in a fog, collapsing
under the weight of mourning as
the world beneath you keeps
spinning. She is you—
you are her. Blindfolded,
ever holding on to the last thread
of hope— aching for
a reason to keep trying, to
keep breathing, to
look up.

// *Hope*, 1879. George Fredric Watts.

IN THE FORM OF AN ANGEL

If only you could hold me
for longer than a moment—
if only you could take more
than my fingertips.
This world is heavy and cruel and
I was never offered wings.
Why must I suffer an icy wind
against my bare skin, cold rocks
beneath my feet— barely able
to lift my head— while you
are given flight and ecstasy and conviction?

Why must I be led or left behind?

I would rather you drop my hands altogether
and leave me alone in this place, than to
look at me like you could love me—
make me feel as if I am yours—
only to, inevitably, leave.

// *Love and Life*, 1895-1904. George Fredric Watts.

THE 'GRACES' REPRESENTED

Do you feel safer? Holding
each other for all time?
Or do you feel exposed,
approached from
all sides— marble
as soft as flesh, do you
fear them getting too close?
Do you fear the touch
of a stranger?
Are you as scared
as I am? Do you think about
how they could pierce through your
stone-walled heart and take advantage— or
do the arms of the women you trust
offer enough solace
and protection?
Tell me— are you afraid?
Are you wary?
Or is it just me— standing
here
before you— exposed—
seen— ignored and wishing
someone would marvel at me
the way we all marvel
at you. They halt, they stare,
and here still, I stand— pen
in hand— absolutely
terrified to look up—
maybe that's why beauty
exists so close to
agony— artists ache
to be seen— to be remembered, and yet,

this rarely happens during their
lifetimes— and
once that day finally
comes around and they
are properly revered—
all that's left are silly
rumors and the same old stories
told again and again until
they lose all semblance of truth.
Mindless scholars
debating for decades over
why they painted the
curtains blue when
that was just the closest
color within reach.
Or maybe their sister
chose— we'll never know.
We wear masks our whole
lives to keep those
around us from ever truly
discovering what happens
inside. How I long to look
into the eyes of an artist and
truly feel what they're feeling.
How I long for someone to look
into mine and not immediately
turn away.

// *The Three Graces*, 1814-17. Antonio Canova.

UNDER THE LIGHT OF THE MOON

With you, Oberon, it's always something more—
it will always be *something* more— a kiss
on the cheek will never only be a kiss on the cheek,
not with you. Your hand holding mine
will *always* set me on fire. I can never
be less than insatiably in love with you.
My heart does not wane away like the phasing
of the moon, it does not wilt in the winter
and hide beneath the earth like those golden
blooms in your hand— my heart is stubbornly
everlasting, more constant than the long-burning lives
of the stars above— and maybe this makes me naive—
for there are still times I doubt your word,
your character, your fidelity— but
I'd rather be naive with a beating heart than
clever with a stone one. Though
the fabric of the universe seems
to unravel every time we touch—
believe me— I pray— despite
the storms that rage and all
that stands between us—
when you are lost— may you
come home, when you are
alone— may you call my name, and
when the rest of this mortal world
makes you question
all that you are made of—
may you look into these eyes, may you
thank those stars above, and more than
anything at all— may you never
doubt our love.

// *The Fairy Lovers*, 1840. Theodor von Holst.

IN SLEEP, OR PERHAPS IN DEATH

Who crumpled you up, dear one?
Who left you behind— on frozen
green onyx and mounds of cold abandonment?
Who made you feel like a forgotten flower
on the kitchen counter— slowly starving
for fresh water— did you bring this
upon yourself? Do you blame
yourself? What burdens weigh
you down? Who have you
lost?
Arms twisted and hands limp—
there is no fire in you.
The darkness is heavy
and you are surrounded.
The sun only rises
for an instant
this time of year—
strangers peer, never
too close. I can't
take it— seeing you this
way tears me apart.
Stand up, please— stand up!
I reach out my hand for
you to hold, but
you can't even lift your head.

// *Snowdrift*, 1901. Edward Onslow Ford.

WHAT IS REAL AND WHAT IS NOT

You stand before a strange world
wrapped in stained linen and
peeling black paint—
the reflections of dark mountains
wade like a threat to light,
a ship's brown carcass
fading from view— just
clear enough to remind
us how close we are
to starvation. Who is going
to ring on this broken
telephone? Your eyes wander
from the two creatures holding
their entire lives on their shoulders, to
the false promise of golden riches, to a
sickly face in the clouds and you wonder
if the old man beside you sees more
than a famous name and
oil paint on canvas— if he feels
the impending mortality
radiating from every
brushstroke. If that
is why he so quickly
walks away.

// *Mountain Lake*, 1938. Salvador Dalí.

HIS SO-CALLED 'ROSE PERIOD'

Madeline, is that really you? Where
have you been? Tell me how can
la vie en rose be so blue?
You gaze out from
your gilded frame, your
indigo cage— looking
onto Caulfield's terrace—
do you wish for an escape?
I will never understand how a
rose period could be so grim—
why a man paints a woman and
forgets about the passion in her
eyes, the dreams in her head.
Are you cold, Madeline? Have
you frozen solid with that icy chemise
as the only hint of protection from
your empty world? Did he ever even
offer you his coat?

// *Girl in a Chemise*, 1905. Pablo Picasso.
// *After Lunch*, 1975. Patrick Caulfield.

THE MUSE, EXTRACTED FROM ANY CONTEXT

I am unfinished, I am torn, I am
left in this room to exist between
the most gorgeous alabaster bather
and the famed beauty
of Psyche herself—
but that does not make me
less.
I may not be soft-spoken, demure,
or perfectly carved— I may be
seamed together and heavy, rough
around the edges, a visage scarred—
but remember— when you look
at them, you only ever see
an ideal of unattainable perfection—
completely out of touch with reality.
When you look at me— you feel
something real. You see something,
someone flawed, broken yet still
standing— more human than
they could ever be.

// *Inner Voice*, 1896. Auguste Rodin.

AN ANGEL SHE CANNOT SEE

From the door to the back wall you
instantly notice something about her
is striking— different— as she peers out
over room 1840— she seems to be
more a part of this world
than her own, as if
she could step
right across her frame and
walk out the door.
Can you imagine? White
chiffon trailing behind, the
scent of madonna lilies, bare feet
padding against cold tile.
Where would she go? To the nearest
high-rise rooftop to feel closer to
her only begotten son? Would
anyone even notice the lone mother
with arms reaching up towards
the heavens— begging
for her God, her Artist—
her Creator— to rescue her?

// *The Annunciation*, 1892. Arthur Hacker.

A STATE OF MELANCHOLY

Don't you understand? Once I begin
loving someone like you— I can't just stop.
You are rooted to my heart in the way
these foolhardy water lilies are
rooted to the soil below. Through
wind and rain, they hold fast.
I look at you and I feel
like I could take flight— but
there are too many things
keeping us apart— too many
reasons why I should
keep my feet on the ground.
I know, I know that we aren't
meant to be— but that doesn't make
the reality of it hurt any less.
All I ever wanted was to walk
beside you in the rain for
days and days— to talk—
to listen— to know you— to learn how
to love you better. To teach you how
to better love me. But now I see that was
foolish and it is time to grow up— to
let these fantasies fade away.
I should have learned from all those
Neverland stories— you were never
going to stay.

// *Disappointed Love*, 1821. Francis Danby.

YELLOW WITH HOPE

You notice the vase looks terribly
similar to an urn, his blooming
and dying held within—
the world fades away to only
soft breath and footsteps—
something about each brushstroke
hurts more and more when
you think of how his most famous starry night
was painted from that east-facing window
of the asylum he checked himself into—
how art is likely the only thing that kept him
alive so long— how someone
so tortured could capture a world
that only ever whispered about him
behind his back— how he made
that sorry town so
tremendously beautiful.
Some say artistry and
madness go hand in hand—
what if art, true art,
must be born from the brink?
What if the only way to make
someone feel anything at all
is for the artist to
(in bravery or lunacy) resign
themselves to an existence of
feeling everything to its absolute
extreme— all at once, all the time.

// *Sunflowers*, 1888. Vincent Van Gogh.

TO FIND HEAVEN

I look out past these pale
blue feathers and in the
distance I can almost
make out the edge of the
world. Wind swirls
through my ears and I can
feel my skin flush pink
against the chilled
atmosphere— the bright
sun all but blinds me
as I blink towards the east—
but this warmth does not melt
my wings. For the first time in
as long as I can remember—
I am free and infinite.

I will always be
more myself when
recklessly reaching for
the scorching stars
than I could ever be
with my feet cautiously
on solid ground.

// *The Sense of Sight*, 1895. Annie Louisa Swynnerton.

EROS CARESSING A BUTTERFLY

From the moment you walked in you knew—
there was nothing you could do to save
this creature from the torment of love—
and why would you?
You know how love can make you feel
more alive and more torn to pieces
than anything else— you know how
you keep trying, keep breaking, keep
trying.
You stand as still as all the other
sculptures in the gallery,
no cautionary words to be said—
your eyes cast down to the
quiver full of arrows and
you remember what it's
like to have a striking, passionate love
pierce its way through your
unsuspecting heart— no
warning— no mercy.
They never told you how
some wounds can never
heal— how some hearts
never beat the same again—
not after him.
Even with all of this
terrible knowing, all of this grief
and pain you carry in your chest—
you still long for another arrow.

// *Love Cherishing the Soul while Preparing to Torment it*, 1837-39. John Gibson.

About the Author

Rachel Clift is a poet, artist, & traveler based in the mountains of East Tennessee. More than anything— she longs to inspire people. This is her first collection of ekphrastic poetry— written in various art museums & galleries around the United Kingdom in February 2022.

She is a firm believer that traveling with only a backpack and little to no plans is the most marvelous thing one can do and no matter how many times a heart may break— it will always keep beating.

RCLIFTPOETRY.COM @R.CLIFTPOETRY

www.ingramcontent.com/pod-product-compliance
Lightning Source LLC
Chambersburg PA
CBHW020916080526
44589CB00011B/621